JAMIE GRACE
ONE SONG AT A TIME

BRENTWOOD-BENSON music publishing in association with TORE RECORDS

CONTENTS

Ready to Fly (Prelude)

Words and Music by
JAMIE GRACE HARPER

Hold Me

Words and Music by
JAMIE GRACE HARPER, TOBY MCKEEHAN
and CHRIS STEVENS

With You

Words and Music by
**JAMIE GRACE HARPER, TOBY MCKEEHAN
and CHRIS STEVENS**

Show Jesus

Words and Music by
GABE PATILLO
and SAM MIZELL

Come to Me

Words and Music by
JAMIE GRACE HARPER
and CHRIS STEVENS

God Girl

Words and Music by
JAMIE GRACE HARPER, TOBY MCKEEHAN
and JAMIE MOORE

48

Holding On

Words and Music by
TOBY MCKEEHAN, JAMIE MOORE,
CARY BARLOWE and MATT HAMMITT

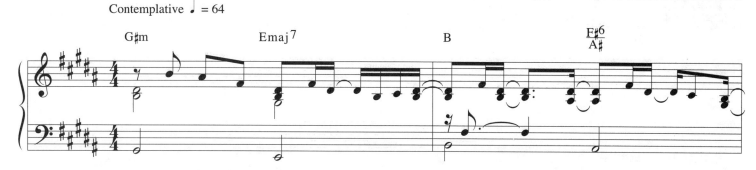

You Lead

Words and Music by
JAMIE GRACE HARPER, TOBY MCKEEHAN,
GABE PATILLO, DAVE WYATT and TIM ROSENAU

One Song at a Time

Words and Music by
JAMIE GRACE HARPER, TOBY MCKEEHAN,
GABE PATILLO and DAVE WYATT

1945

Words and Music by
JAMIE GRACE HARPER
and CHRIS STEVENS

Reggae feel, shuffle ♩ = 140

Look-in' at the ra-di-o, caught up in a dream___ 'bout the days gone by___ when no one had a T. V.___

Not Alone

**Words and Music by
JAMIE GRACE HARPER**

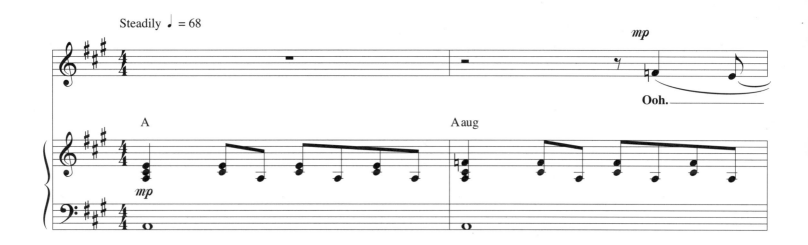

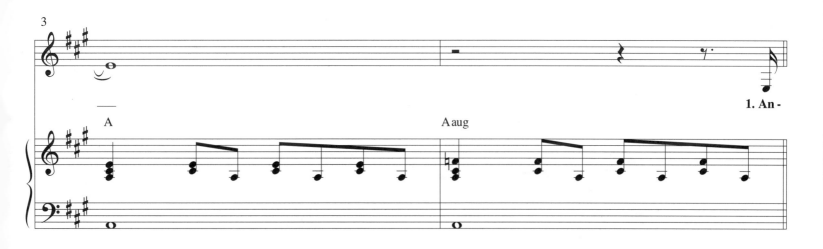

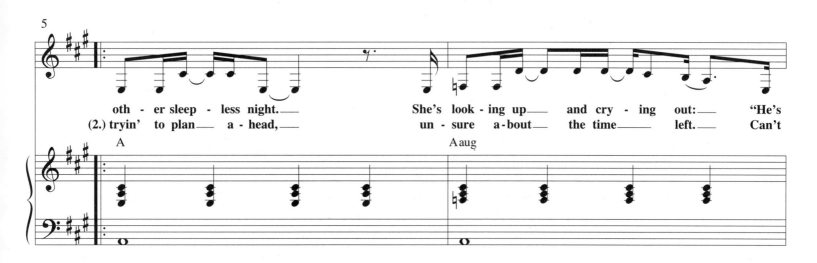